Taxes, Taxes!

Where the Money Goes

by Nancy Loewen * illustrated by Brad Fitzpatrick

Thanks to our advisers for their expertise, research, and advice:

Dr. Joseph Santos
Associate Professor of Economics, Department of Economics
South Dakota State University

Susan Kesselring, M.A., Literacy Educator
Rosemount–Apple Valley–Eagan (Minnesota) School District

PICTURE WINDOW BOOKS
Minneapolis, Minnesota

Editorial Director: Carol Jones
Managing Editor: Catherine Neitge
Creative Director: Keith Griffin
Editor: Christianne Jones
Story Consultant: Terry Flaherty
Designer: Joe Anderson
Page Production: Picture Window Books
The illustrations in this book were created digitally.

Picture Window Books
5115 Excelsior Boulevard
Suite 232
Minneapolis, MN 55416
877-845-8392
www.picturewindowbooks.com

Printed in the United States of America.

Library of Congress Cataloging-in-Publication Data
Loewen, Nancy, 1964-
Taxes, taxes! : where the money goes / written by Nancy
Loewen ; illustrated by Brad Fitzpatrick.
p. cm. — (Money matters)
Includes bibliographical references and index.
ISBN 1-4048-1158-3 (hard cover)
1. Taxation—United States—Juvenile
literature. 2. Taxation—Juvenile literature.
I. Fitzpatrick, Brad, ill. II. Title. III. Money
matters (Minneapolis, Minn.)

HJ2381.T638 2006
336.2'00973—dc22   2005004065

Ms. Colby asked her class of third graders, "Tell me what the following things have in common: a highway, a library book, a park, a soldier's salary. Think about who pays for these things. Where does the money come from?"

Several hands shot into the air.

"Sharon, what do you think?" Ms. Colby asked.

"Taxes!" Sharon said. "All of those things are paid for by the government with money from taxes."

"Right!" Ms. Colby said. "Our government collects money, or taxes, from people and businesses. Then, the government spends that money on goods and services that benefit everyone."

Taxes existed even before money did. In Ancient Mesopotamia, people were required to bring cows and sheep to the tax collectors.

Ms. Colby asked the class to brainstorm about the ways tax dollars are spent. She wrote their ideas on the board. Pretty soon, the entire board was full!

5

How Taxes are Spent

› Community workers like fire fighters, rescue squads, and police officers

› Public schools, libraries, parks, transportation, and buildings

› Building and fixing roads and bridges

› Plowing and sanding highways and city streets

› School needs—paying teachers and staff, buying books, supplies, and computers

› Keeping public water safe

› Making sure food in restaurants and grocery stores is safe

› Making sure medicines are safe

› Helping people who have been through a natural disaster— tornadoes, earthquakes, floods, hurricanes, and droughts

› Court systems, jails, and prisons

› Social Security—providing income for retired people, disabled people, and orphans

› National defense—military branches like the Army, Navy, Marines, Airforce, and Coast Guard

› Helping other countries

Ms. Colby explained, "There are three main levels of government: federal, state, and local. The federal government is national and affects everyone living in the United States. However, it doesn't control everything. The states have a lot of power. The states, in turn, give a lot of power to cities and counties."

People who don't pay their taxes are breaking the law.

"So people pay taxes to all three?" Philip asked.

"In one way or another, yes," Ms. Colby replied. "I'm going to let someone else tell you more about that. We've got a surprise guest today!"

Todd's mom came into the classroom.

"This is Mrs. O'Brien. She has an important job with the IRS," Ms. Colby said.

In the year 2000, the IRS collected more than $2 trillion from 226 million tax returns.

10

Mrs. O'Brien took over. "IRS stands for Internal Revenue Service. It's the agency in charge of collecting federal taxes. Internal means within the United States. Revenue is a fancy word for the tax dollars the government receives," she said.

"Who wants to ask the first question?" Mrs. O'Brien asked.

"Me!" said Jamie. "Who decides how much people pay in taxes?"

"Well," said Mrs. O'Brien, "citizens elect senators and representatives who make bills, or proposed tax laws. Then, the president or governor signs them into law. On the local level, people often vote directly on tax issues. If we don't think our taxes are fair, we can vote for someone we think will do a better job."

Taxation was one of the issues that led to the Revolutionary War.

Kelby asked, "What kind of taxes are there? And which part of the government gets which taxes?"

"The federal government gets most of its money from income taxes. Every year, people who earn money need to report their income to the government. They have to pay part of their income to the United States Treasury. That process is called filing a tax return," Ms. Colby said.

People pay income taxes at different rates, depending on their incomes. Those who earn a lot of money pay a higher percentage than those who don't earn as much.

14

FEDERAL GOVERNMENT

STATE GOVERNMENT

"Don't people pay income tax to states, too?" asked Audrey.

"In most states, yes," answered Mrs. O'Brien. "However, not every state collects income taxes."

"States also raise money through sales taxes," Ms. Colby said. "A sales tax is an extra charge that you pay when you buy something. Many cities have sales taxes, too."

The average sales tax, including both state and local taxes, is 6.25 percent.

"State and local governments also have user fees. These only apply to the people who are actually using a government service. If you buy a fishing license, you're helping to support programs that keep lakes healthy and stocked with fish," she said.

"I've heard my parents talk about property taxes," said Ryan. "What are those?"

"Property taxes are based on the value of a person's home or land and collected by local governments," Mrs. O'Brien said. "These fees have to be paid every year. It's not just individuals—businesses have to pay property taxes, too. A lot of that money goes to pay for public schools. It also pays for things like police officers, fire fighters, streets, sewers, and parks."

Renters pay rent to landlords. The landlords use some of the money to pay property taxes.

"Tax revenues are always moving," Mrs. O'Brien said. "While a school gets money from local property taxes, it also receives money from state and federal governments. In return, the teachers and staff pay sales taxes on what they buy, property taxes on their homes, and income taxes every year. It all goes around and around. The goal of a tax system is to create balance, so that all people have their basic needs met."

Ms. Colby stood up. "Speaking of basic needs, it's time for lunch. Thanks, Mrs. O'Brien!"

The Revenue Act of 1942 required employers to withhold taxes from employee's paychecks. This created a regular flow of money that was used to pay the costs of World War II.

21

The Government and You

Households, businesses, and the government all connect. When you pay taxes, the government uses some of the money for services and payments for businesses. In turn, the businesses employ people, giving them income, which they spend and are taxed on. Follow the arrows in the circular diagram to see how everything connects.

Fun Facts

- Taxpayers have a right to privacy. No one except authorized tax personnel can look at a person's tax return.

- The first time the U.S. government required people to pay income tax was in 1862. The money was used to pay for the Civil War.

- For most individuals, federal and state tax returns are due April 15 every year.

- Lawmakers often use taxes as a way to influence people's behavior. Luxury taxes apply to very expensive cars and other costly items. Gasoline taxes encourage people to conserve energy and are used to build roads and mass transportation systems.

- People can now file their tax returns over the Internet.

Glossary

benefit—to be helped by something

elect—to choose by voting

federal government—the central government of the United States

goods—things that can be bought or sold

lawmakers—elected officials who make laws

luxury—something not really needed

Mesopotamia—an area in southwestern Asia between the Tigris and Euphrates rivers in what is now Iraq

representatives—people who speak or act for others

revenue—money made by a government from taxes

senators—a member of the senate

services—work that helps others, such as providing medical care, fixing cars, or cutting hair

To Learn More

At the Library

De Capua, Sarah. *Paying Taxes*. New York: Children's Press, 2002.

Giesecke, Ernestine. *Your Money at Work: Taxes*. Chicago: Heinemann Library, 2003.

On the Web

FactHound offers a safe, fun way to find Web sites related to this book. All of the sites on FactHound have been researched by our staff. *www.facthound.com*

1. Visit the FactHound home page.

2. Enter a search word related to this book, or type in this special code: 1404811583

3. Click on the FETCH IT button.

Your trusty FactHound will fetch the best sites for you!

Look for all of the books in the Money Matters series:

DISCARD